P9-DES-079

SAN FRANCISCO
VICTORIANS

SAN FRANCISCO
VICTORIANS

PHOTOGRAPHS BY
Michael Blumensaadt

ESSAY BY
Randolph Delehanty

CHRONICLE BOOKS
SAN FRANCISCO

In memory of
Albert J. Moorman

Photographs copyright © 2000 by Michael Blumensaadt.

Text copyright © 2000 by Randolph Delehanty.

Library of Congress Cataloging-in-Publication Data available.

ISBN 0-8118-2771-2

Printed in Singapore.

Book and cover design by John Sullivan and Dennis Gallagher, Visual Strategies

Distributed in Canada by
Raincoast Books
8680 Cambie Street
Vancouver, British Columbia V6P 6M9

10 9 8 7 6 5 4 3 2 1

Chronicle Books
85 Second Street
San Francisco, California 94105

www.chroniclebooks.com

Contents

6   PREFACE

8   DELIRIUM IN WOOD
Essay by Randolph Delehanty

32   PHOTOGRAPHS

Early Styles — 32
Italianate Style — 40
Eastlake Style — 66
Queen Anne Style — 98
Late Styles — 126

134   LEARNING MORE

137   VISITOR'S GUIDE

143   ABOUT THE PHOTOGRAPHER AND AUTHOR

Preface

I FIRST CAME to San Francisco in the late 1960s during the heyday of Urban Renewal, when the city's Victorian houses were undervalued and under attack. I remember walking through the vacated blocks of the boarded-up Western Addition wondering at the madness of destroying this unique architectural ensemble and replacing it with sterile stucco buildings that didn't even have the city sense to fence in their backyards. I determined to use my historical training to help San Franciscans understand what they had and why it was worth holding onto and restoring. My years as the first historian for San Francisco Architectural Heritage from 1973 to 1978 were rewarding. We were part of a gathering wave of appreciation for what is unique about this city, both physically and socially. Eventually a combination of neighborhood height limits, a resurgent Bay Area economy, and new people who saw old buildings in imaginative ways rescued the city's vintage houses. Today it is almost impossible to find a shabby Victorian house in all of San Francisco.

San Francisco's wooden Victorian row houses proved to be surprisingly adaptable over time. Many have come full circle in their hundred plus years from middle-class, single-family houses to being broken up into rooming houses or apartments, and back again to single-family dwellings. Their syncopated pattern of bay windows delights the eye; their just-right density creates sociable neighborhoods; they are land- and energy-efficient; and they link us with our rich history. Today people come from all over the world to climb our hilly streets and to enjoy the exuberance of our Victorian heritage. This little book celebrates the rediscovery of these architectural gems. I trust that it pleases those who live here and those who visit the Golden Gate city. *Visitor's Guide: Select Northern California Historic Houses* on page 137 lists house museums where you can experience the interiors of these splendid survivors.

—*Randolph Delehanty*
San Francisco

Delirium in Wood

›‹◆›‹

WHEN SILVER WAS discovered under the treeless hills of western Nevada, San Francisco went wild in an orgy of stock speculation. While everyone has heard of the Gold Rush of 1849 that put California on the map, most of that wealth ended up in New York City or London; very little of it stayed in frontier San Francisco. But the Comstock silver bonanza was different; much of the wealth extracted from the Nevada mines was invested in, or was spent in, San Francisco. Here it funded banks and insurance companies, built great hotels and fancy restaurants, patronized luxury shops—and produced showy architecture. Land speculation and building took off. Investors bought sandy blocks or lots and erected commercial and residential buildings during the heady boom. The good times peaked in 1868–69, to be followed by a sharp bust that lasted four years.

In 1874 another wild expansion took place, spurred by a second bonanza of Nevada silver. It lasted until 1877. By the 1870s, California was well integrated into the world economy, and it fell into the severe, worldwide Great Depression that lingered from 1878 to 1884. Building slowed and real estate values in the Golden Gate city shrank by one-quarter to one-third. The late 1870s were a time of acute political tension in San Francisco, with white workers scapegoating the Chinese for the drastic fall in wages.

Good times roared back in 1885. San Francisco grew rich exporting the tidal wave of wheat from the great Central Valley. By then, cable car lines were reaching out from the downtown and radiating over the hilly peninsula, opening up once inaccessible hilltops and distant valleys for new housing. An especially great wave of speculative building took place all over California in 1886. Some of the most exuberant Victorians ever built were confected during this giddy peak of economic and architectural extravagance. This spurt of growth lasted until 1893, when a second worldwide

depression hit California. Building slacked off until another revival in 1899 triggered a sustained boom that closed the century and lasted until 1906.

These pulses of boom and bust help explain the succession of architectural styles in nineteenth-century San Francisco. Generally speaking, every time building rebounded it did so in a new style.

While the full story is more complex than this brief introduction can sketch (see photographer Richard Sexton's and my *In the Victorian Style* for a more extensive history, including interiors), San Francisco participated in the international architectural trends of the second half of the nineteenth century. Architectural styles also overlapped in the nineteenth century. While some people were building houses in the latest style, others were more conservative and clung to past fashions. Some houses combined more than one style, especially in the mid-1880s, when the Eastlake style fused with the emerging Queen Anne style.

THE SAN FRANCISCO ROW HOUSE

THE EARLIEST HOUSES in Gold Rush San Francisco were plain clapboard, freestanding dwellings crowded together around the harbor. As the port boomed, city surveyors laid out a series of grids over the steeply hilly site heedless of the shape of the land. Speculators and homestead associations bought these blocks and subdivided them into narrow house lots, generally 25 feet wide and 100 feet deep. On these constricted sites builders shoehorned long, narrow wood houses that came out almost to the sidewalk but left a small yard to the rear. Tall board fences secured their backyards.

The first row houses in San Francisco were built in 1854 by London-born George Gordon. His elite, block-square South Park development of stucco-covered brick party-wall houses followed West End London precedents and featured a private oval park around which the houses were arranged. Local builders took this compact row-house form, dropped the expensive park, and built in wood rather than costly brick. San Francisco's two-story row houses are actually freestanding; they do not share party walls with their neighbors.

The challenge in designing these houses was getting light and air into the rooms in the middle of the building. This was solved by the introduction of a "slot" along one side of the narrow house that pulled back to the middle of the building. The dining room, a room that does not need direct sunlight, was placed in the center of the first floor, the darkest part of the house. A service alley passed under the dining room's side bay window, giving access to the back of the lot. This "slot" seems to have been a San Francisco invention. No one knows who came up with the idea.

A standard floor plan quickly evolved that placed a long, narrow hall on the side opposite the "slot" with a staircase giving access to the second floor. Rooms branched off the long hallway on both floors. A formal front parlor with a bay window, an informal second parlor, and a dining room, pantry, and kitchen occupied the first floor from front to back. Pairs of pocket doors connected the first-floor rooms. On the second floor were the master bedroom in front with a bay window, a sitting room, and two to three smaller bedrooms in the back. The separate water closet (toilet) and bathroom were often placed halfway back on the second floor. Back stairs connected the upstairs rear with the first floor.

Most San Francisco row houses did not have full basements; they were simply raised up off the damp ground on brick footings. Roofs were usually flat and had no attics (rain is infrequent in San Francisco). Most Victorian San Franciscans did not keep horses or carriages; they used the city's dense network of cable car lines and later, electric streetcars. Row houses were an efficient, and profitable, way to build city houses. Often these houses were built in groups to further reduce construction costs. While exterior decoration and bay window shapes changed with the whims of fashion, the basic form of the row house lasted from the 1860s into the early twentieth century. Showier houses were usually built only on large, prestigious corner lots.

THE SUCCESSION OF STYLES

The Greek Revival

THE VICTORIAN PERIOD began in California in the late 1840s with simple, almost "styleless," wooden houses. In the 1850s the chaste Greek Revival style, which is found in New England, upstate New York, the Midwest, and across the antebellum South, appeared throughout remote California. Classic Greek temples with their stately columns inspired the style. In pioneer California these were often simple box columns without elaborately carved capitals. While public buildings were built in stone, or stucco-covered

brick scored to look like stone, wood Greek Revival buildings were the most common. Both public Greek Revival buildings and houses were generally sober and symmetrical. Rooms were usually rectangular and building plans quite simple. Only a few of these buildings survive in San Francisco, in the Mission District and at Fort Mason and the Presidio.

The Gothic Revival

THE STOLID GREEK REVIVAL was followed by the more fanciful Gothic Revival, with its pointed arch windows and delight in turrets and a picturesque "skyline" (the profile of the building seen against the sky). Some Gothic Revival mansions were built in San Francisco

with Nevada silver or transcontinental railroad millions. The most fantastic of them all was the Mark Hopkins mansion of 1878 that crowned Nob Hill with a riot of towers and elaborate chimneys. It made a crackling bonfire in 1906. Very few Gothic Revival houses survive in San Francisco. In the California countryside simplified Gothic Revival farmhouses with steeply pitched roofs, hooded dormers, and windows with pointed arch tops survive here and there. The romantic Gothic Revival style never died in the United States. It became the preferred style for Christian churches and collegiate ivory towers.

The Italianate Style

AS THE GOTHIC REVIVAL peaked another historicist style grew up alongside it, what we now call the Italianate style. Especially popular in the booming Silver Seventies, the Italianate style claimed to have its stylistic roots in the robust, high-style stone buildings of the Italian Renaissance in its mannerist phase. It was first popularized by some of the Pall Mall men's clubs in London and then imitated in America. Occasionally built of stone or stucco-covered brick, in San Francisco the Italianate style was adopted for the proliferating middle-class row houses, almost all of which were built of wood. Grand houses, often with square towers, were called Italian villas. The grandest survivor of the type is the brownstone Flood mansion atop Nob Hill, now the Pacific-Union Club, a late example designed in 1886 by Augustus Laver and restored and enlarged in 1909.

A distinguishing feature of Italianate design was the use of quoins, blocks of wood placed along the edges of facades in imitation of corner stonework. Woodworking mills south of Market Street poured out an avalanche of ornamental trim, stock windows, doors, cornices, and overmantels. This was the period when bay windows became popular in San Francisco. Italianate bay windows usually had three equal-sized  windows with the two side windows placed at an angle. Many Italianate row houses were built in San Francisco in the 1870s, and quite a few have survived.

The Eastlake, or Stick, Style

NEXT, IN THE 1880s, yet another style appeared in Great Britain, on the East Coast, and in distant California. Rooted in the conscious reform of furniture design and domestic interiors, and animated by opposition to the Gothic Revival, this style took its name from the London furniture designer and popular writer Sir Charles Lock Eastlake (though Eastlake himself, when told of the houses being built in California and called "Eastlake," was appalled by them). Eastlake

houses have a marked angularity. They often have right-angled decorative woodwork and seem to express their underlying wood frame construction through their nailed-on exterior decoration. This is what gives them the nick-name "Stick style." Ornament is sometimes incised, that is, carved *into* the surface of the wood rather than projecting out from it. The Eastlake style was part of the Aesthetic Movement in England and in the Anglophile United States. Eastlake houses could be simple or wildly fanciful.

Bay windows in the 1880s went from slant-sided to rectangular in plan. This made the bays larger and more useful from within.

Eastlake houses of the late 1880s were often exuberantly orna-mented. It was then that true architectural delirium was achieved.

The taste for varied room shapes, asymmetrical exteriors, and rich ornament reached a crescendo. This was the heyday of new mechanical inventions for woodworking, and mill operators published catalogs advertising just about every possibility in the manipulation of soft redwood. Brackets, columns, window frames, doors, and cornices became almost mannerist in mood. Exaggeration, invention, fancy—these were what home buyers craved in the 1880s. These were the houses that later generations were to brand "monstrosities" and eagerly pull down. But to our contemporary postmodern taste, lately freed from the puritanism of the Modern Movement, it is just these designs that captivate and delight. (Just what *is* that bracket doing? And that column: what's with all the knobs and rings? And that capital? What order is *that*?)

A few Eastlake houses incorporated round corner towers. The best surviving example is the Haas-Lilienthal house in Pacific Heights, designed by Peter R. Schmidt in 1886 and today the home of San Francisco Architectural Heritage (see pages 9 and 141).

The Queen Anne Style

THE EASTLAKE STYLE was followed in San Francisco by what is locally called the Queen Anne style, which is not the same style as eighteenth-century English Queen Anne furniture and silver or Richard Norman Shaw's medievalized nineteenth-century architecture in England. Designs became somewhat more controlled, at least in comparison with the wild manipulations of the late 1880s. Fash-

ionable in the late 1880s and 1890s, these new houses delighted in varied room shapes and grand interior plans. They often employed a variety of materials on their exteriors including intricately patterned shingle work and fancy plasterwork. Curves now appeared in round corner towers, semicircular or three-quarter-circle bay windows, and arched entrances. Ornament started to become more "classical," that is, based on motifs from ancient Greece

and Rome. Decorative woodwork became less angular than that of the Aesthetic taste of the Eastlake style. Laurel wreaths, flowing ribbons, and flaming torches were favorite Queen Anne decorative touches. There was a steady movement toward control and refinement. In San Francisco, Queen Anne houses brought back gable roofs, succeeding the flat roofs of the earlier Italianate and Eastlake houses. Luxurious Queen Anne houses favored round corner towers with curved glass windows, a new and ostentatious invention. One neighborhood that was building in the 1890s was the Haight-

Ashbury near Golden Gate Park, and many Queen Anne row houses still line its streets. Large Queen Anne houses are also found in Pacific Heights.

The Shingle Style and Other Styles

NINETEENTH-CENTURY architects ransacked the world looking for ideas and ornament. Many minor architectural styles surfaced during the Victorian era, from the Moorish Revival to the Romanesque Revival to Swiss chalets. The most impressive was the French Second Empire style with its mansard roofs and pompous splendor. It was generally reserved for great public buildings, important institutions, and especially ostentatious mansions.

The late nineteenth-century style with the most important afterlife in northern California was the Shingle style. Originating in England and New England, this style found favor among a handful of San Francisco's educated elite in the 1890s. From it evolved the small but influential cluster of shingle houses on Russian Hill and Presidio Heights and the greater number of rustic dwellings in the bosky Berkeley hills and other country places. These "natural"

houses with their relaxed plans, and a handful of small, inventive churches, became the seed from which a distinctive Bay Area architectural tradition blossomed in the twentieth century. They were a reaction to the excesses of the Gilded Age, though they could be quite luxuriously appointed. There were never very many Shingle style houses in late Victorian San Francisco.

The Colonial and Classical Revivals

AS THE NINETEENTH CENTURY came to a close there emerged on the East Coast what architects called the Colonial Revival. High-style

designers looked back at Georgian buildings in places like Newport, Rhode Island, and other eighteenth-century Atlantic ports and admired their elegance and restraint. The visual lightness of their ornament and the quieter outlines of the buildings themselves made them the new model of Good Taste. These Colonial Revival houses, of which there are only a few in San Francisco, exude a sense of calm and refinement.

In 1901, Queen Victoria's sixty-four-year reign came to an end. She was succeeded by her son, Edward VII, who reigned from 1901 to

1910. The Edwardian decade was characterized by the drier designs of the Classical Revival and Beaux-Arts styles.

The Big Picture

IF WE STEP back and look at the full sweep of house design in Victorian San Francisco, we see the simple houses of the Greek Revival succeeded by the romantic Gothic Revival and then the heavier Italianate Mannerist styles. They in turn are succeeded by the robust, confident, even brash Eastlake houses of the 1880s, which reached their peak of elaboration about 1886. After that, in the Queen Annes, designs quiet down, until, by the Classical Revival of the Edwardian period, sobriety triumphs and the exuberance of the late Victorians becomes an embarrassment to their children. Underneath the changing froth of styles was an economic, enduring house type—the two-story frame row house—which accounted for the vast majority of San Francisco houses throughout the nineteenth century and well into the twentieth century.

The Surviving Victorian Crescent

THE EARTHQUAKE OF April 18, 1906, triggered three days of fires that devastated the Victorian downtown and the older inner-city neighborhoods. The conflagration destroyed the core of the commercial and residential city including the entire downtown, China-town, most of Telegraph and Russian Hills, all of Nob Hill, North Beach, South of Market, and the Inner Mission District. But San Francisco was still the premier city on the Pacific Coast when catastrophe struck. Also, this was the first insured catastrophe, and the city had the ready capital with which to rebuild quickly. The new Edwardian city was rebuilt in a restrained, classically influenced style.

The fire of 1906 left a crescent of surviving Victorian houses in wealthy Pacific Heights, the middle-class Western Addition, Haight-Ashbury, the Castro, Noe Valley, part of the working-class Mission District, and the lightly built Potrero District. With the exception of an east-west swath of the low-lying Victorian Western Addition that was demolished by Urban Renewal in the 1960s and 1970s, these Victorian neighborhoods survive today. In the early and mid-twentieth century there was still enough undeveloped land in the city for new neighborhoods to develop farther to the west and south of this historic crescent.

Victorians Become "Monstrosities"

ATTITUDES TOWARDS Victorian houses have changed over time. The correct academic taste of the Beaux-Arts in the early twentieth century, the revival styles of the 1920s (in California, the Mission

SAN FRANCISCO VICTORIAN NEIGHBORHOODS TODAY

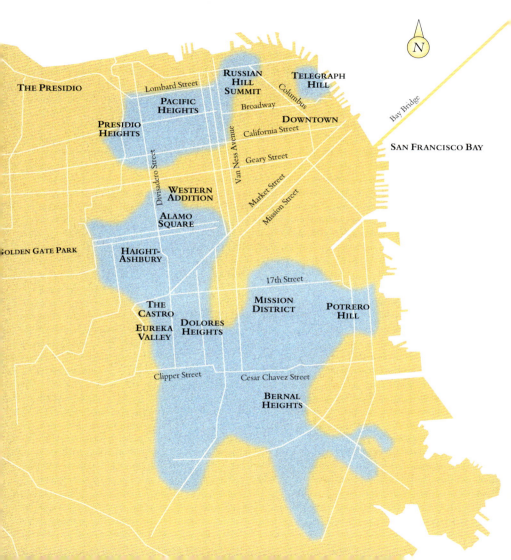

style especially), modernist Art Deco, and then the severe Modern Movement, were all very different. All they had in common was deep distaste, hatred even, for Victorian "monstrosities." The otherwise excellent guidebook to San Francisco produced by the WPA in the late 1930s looked with horror at these ornate, ungainly, to them, dark houses. When building resumed in the late 1940s after the hiatus of World War II, no one thought twice about razing Victorian houses for modern buildings or even parking lots. So-called Urban Renewal in the late 1960s and early 1970s had a positive hatred not just of ornamented nineteenth-century buildings but even of the blocks they sat on. Hundreds of Victorians were demolished in the then-poor and African-American Western Addition to make way for consolidated super blocks with modern "garden apartments." The lowest point was reached when the San Francisco Fire Department set an Italianate Victorian row house on fire to practice fire fighting. The city's old houses were not regarded as heirlooms; they were just junk in the way of Progress. And they were momentarily cheap.

An important cultural shift occurred after this orgy of architectural cleansing. America, a society that is almost unbelievably mobile, restless even, and fundamentally future-oriented, began to look back at its nineteenth-century past with indulgent nostalgia.

There are both negative and positive reasons for this. The negative reason is that most of the new America built after the 1940s was flat and featureless. The avant-garde Modern Movement and the corporate International Style, so brilliant when in the hands of masters like Le Corbusier or Mies van der Rohe, became soul destroying in the hands of bottom-line speculative developers. Endless flat roofs and blank walls began to look bleak, not chic. The banishment of all architectural ornament as some kind of aesthetic crime filled our cities and suburban shopping centers with faceless buildings that offered nothing to the hungry eye except overscaled, brightly lit signs. All sense of craft vanished. Rooms had no moldings and windows were trimmed with minimal aluminum frames. Paneled doors disappeared and became flat slabs. The aesthetic puritans in alliance with the sharp-pencil cost-cutters banished all delight, all "mere decoration." Apartments and houses with no vestibules, low ceilings, no trim, no bay windows, no porches, no towers, almost no nothing, proliferated. High-rises became standing cereal boxes; shopping centers were cereal boxes laid on their side. Gaping, doorless garages disrupted the continuity of the pedestrian's sidewalk. A stray palm tree or two in a planter out front, or a potted rubber plant in a sterile lobby, could not redeem these new, alienating environments.

The Victorian Revival

THE POSITIVE SIDE of the late-1970s' changes in attitude was the rediscovery of vintage buildings, walkable streetcar neighborhoods, and historic cities by a suburban-bred, college-educated generation.

This was a popular revolt, not one preached in architecture and design schools. (They clung to the intellectually superior Modernist faith.) In city planning, the unorthodox ideas of Jane Jacobs, not a professional city planner, caught on with the unhappy public. In architecture and interior decoration a taste for the old and funky erupted. The San Francisco hippies were part of this aesthetic revolt against "pure," sterile, modern design. Haight-Ashbury interiors became jungles of old furniture, thrift store bric-a-brac, and self-made psychedelic art. Even old clothing made a comeback for a brief Neo-Romantic moment. The very late 1960s and early 1970s were also a time when certain neighborhoods in San Francisco, almost all of them built in the Victorian era, were in decline as new home buyers gravitated to the expanding suburbs. City rents and house prices dropped. Urban homesteaders, many of them gay men, began to buy old buildings to fix them up and sell them for a profit, using the proceeds to continue the process with another faded Victorian on a slightly less desirable block. The mid-1970s were the watershed; house prices in San Francisco began to escalate dramatically. Childless couples realized that they could buy an old Victorian house, restore the fanciful exterior, update the utilities, rework the interior with new kitchens, baths, back decks, and skylights, insert a garage under the building, and live a rich life close to the heart of the city. About this time once-cheap undeveloped suburban land began to disappear in the booming Bay Area. Commutes got longer as the region expanded and living in town became more attractive. The Victorian revival gained momentum among the middle class. Almost overnight, it seemed, old buildings became all the rage.

The "Painted Ladies"

THE TRADITIONAL COLORS for nineteenth-century San Francisco houses were white, gray, and occasionally, brown. There were some two-tone color schemes in the Victorian era where the body of the building was painted perhaps medium brown and the raised woodwork dark brown. The window sash (the narrow wood frame that holds the glass) was often painted black, dark green, or

deep red. In the early twentieth century, light beige, sometimes referred to as "landlady's beige," was widely popular. It was less expensive and more practical to paint wooden houses all in one light-reflecting color that faded evenly.

At first the urban homesteaders, in their urge to stake their turf and proclaim the rebirth of old houses, and influenced by the psychedelic art of the hippies, took to painting their Victorians garish colors. In the early 1970s one vividly painted house in the Western

Addition was made into a popular postcard and the trend accelerated. (That particular house had a fake alligator nailed to its second-story exterior, an idea that mercifully never caught on.) Sometimes every ornamental element was picked out in bright primary colors. Pairs of columns were sometimes painted different colors, something no trained architect would have done. In many cases these "restorations" were only skin deep. Changing the color from the traditional gray or beige was just a way to "flip" the hyped real estate. Neighborhoods began to develop distinctive color schemes. The brightest colors were in the overstimulated Haight-Ashbury. More restrained approaches to color predominated in establishment Pacific Heights.

After this burst of experimentation came the professionalization of house color selection in San Francisco. "Color consultants" emerged, who did not themselves paint the houses but who picked new color schemes for new home owners. While their colors were less wild than the first new color combinations, these colorists of the 1980s also liked to use many strong colors. A series of popular books promoted these "painted ladies," usually showing individual, highly colored houses seen in isolation. Their disruptive effect on the traditional pale streetscape was ignored. "San Francisco colors" were copied all over the country as the

preservation movement spread into the hinterland. Colors that had never been popular in San Francisco, such as royal blue, dark purple, and occasionally even black, appeared. But San Francisco's California light is strong, harsh even, and these multicolor schemes faded unevenly and soon became blotchy and unsightly. They were also, of course, more expensive than simple paint jobs. It turned out that there was a practical reason why "landlady beige" was the traditional color in San Francisco: light colors fade more slowly and more evenly, and their eventually chalky surfaces reflect and soften the hard California light. San Francisco is a white, light-reflecting city when seen from a distance, not a dark one.

House Colors Today

As VICTORIANS ACHIEVED popularity with wealthier buyers, Good Taste began to assert itself. Now new owners of thoroughly restored old houses sought to blend in with their revived neighborhoods, not aggressively stand out from them. A happy medium evolved using a three-color (or four-color) paint scheme. The raised ornamental woodwork framing the doors, windows, porch, and cornice was painted white or cream. The body of the building (the plain clapboard) was painted a soft but pleasing color, perhaps warm tan or dove gray. The base of the building was painted that same color but in a darker shade, dark tan or a dark gray. The fourth color, when used, was sparingly applied and reserved for the narrow band of the window sash. It was always the strongest color in the new paint scheme, perhaps a very dark red with the tan house or black for the gray house. There was a turn away from aggressively dark colors, which tend to disrupt the visual continuity of rows of city houses. Paint schemes became more "neighbor friendly" as inner-city neighborhoods became uniformly middle-class again.

A final touch came in the late 1990s as San Francisco Victorians became almost worth their weight in gold: here and there pieces of exterior ornament were accented with gold paint or even had real gold leaf applied to them. This is something even the Victorians of 1886 would have considered over the top. But these precious flourishes accurately reflect the now elevated status of meticulously restored Victorian houses in the opulent San Francisco of today, a time of irrational exuberance almost as fervid as the Silver Seventies, when our story began.

Early Styles

Telegraph Hill

➢ Telegraph Hill

Mission District

Mission District

Pacific Heights

Presidio/GGNRA

Italianate Style

*Pacific
Heights*

Pacific Heights

Western Addition

Pacific Heights

Pacific Heights

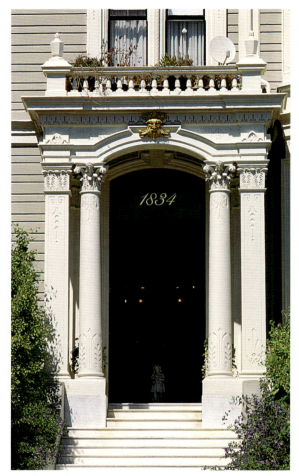

Pacific Heights

➤ *Pacific Heights*

Pacific Heights

➤ *Dolores Heights*

◄ *Pacific Heights*

Pacific Heights

◄ *Western Addition*

Western Addition

Pacific Heights

Overleaf:
Western Addition

Pacific Heights

➤ *Dolores Heights*

Nob Hill

Nob Hill

Pacific Heights

Pacific Heights

Pacific Heights

Pacific Heights

Eastlake Style

Haight-Ashbury

Western Addition

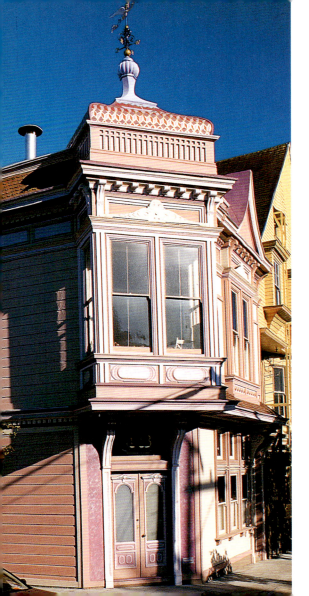

The Castro

Pacific Heights

Western Addition

Western Addition

Western Addition

Nob Hill

➤ *Western Addition*

Pacific Heights

Pacific Heights

Western Addition

Alamo Square

The Castro

The Castro

Dolores Heights

<= *Pacific Heights*

Pacific Heights

Pacific Heights

The Castro

Haight-Ashbury

Pacific Heights

Pacific Heights

Pacific Heights

The Castro

➤ *The Castro*

The Castro   ➢ *Pacific Heights*

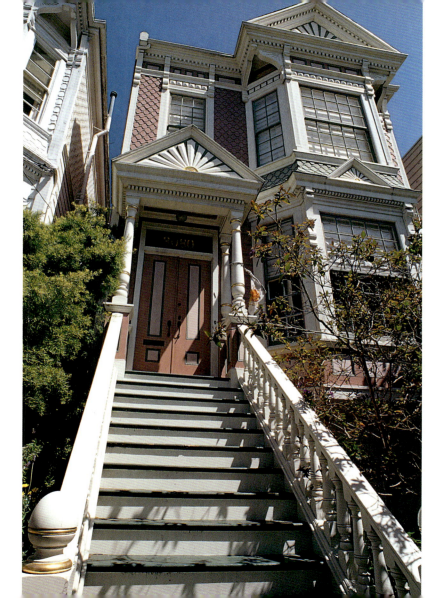

The Castro

The Castro

Queen Anne Style

Haight-Ashbury

Western Addition

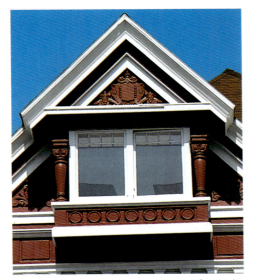

Pacific Heights

Haight-Ashbury

Eureka Valley

Alamo Square

➤ *Haight-Ashbury*

Alamo Square

Alamo Square

Haight-Ashbury

➢ *Western Addition*

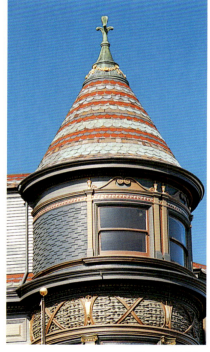

Western Addition

Western Addition

Alamo Square

Overleaf:
Western Addition

Pacific Heights

≺ Pacific Heights

Pacific Heights

Western Addition

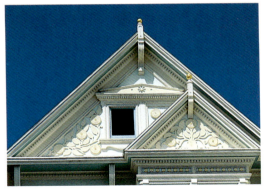

Pacific Heights

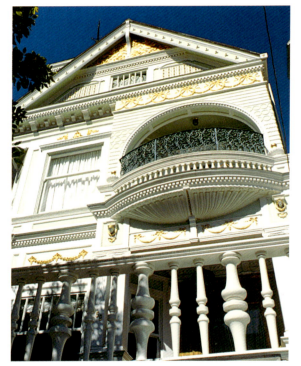

Haight-Ashbury ➤ *Alamo Square*

Overleaf:
Pacific Heights

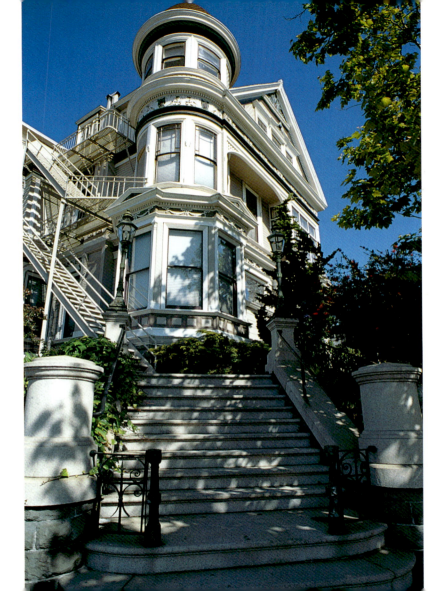

Pacific Heights

≺ *Pacific Heights*

Overleaf:
Western Addition

Presidio Heights

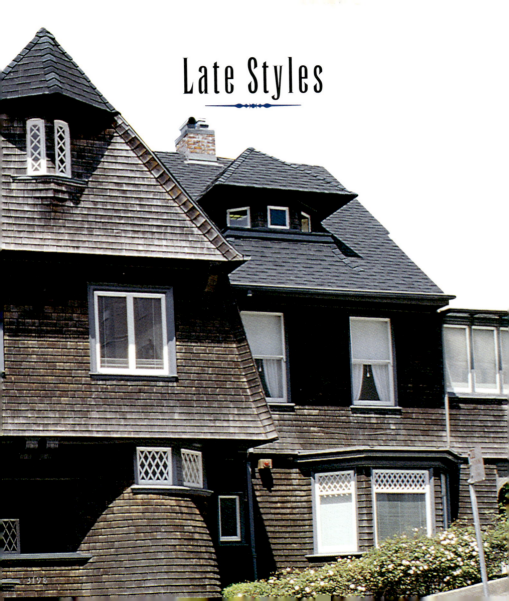

Late Styles

Presidio Heights

Van Ness Avenue

Dolores Heights

Overleaf:
Dolores Heights

The Victorian
era came to a close
in 1901. In the
succeeding Edwardian
period many flats
and apartments were
built incorporating
classical details and
bay windows. These
Edwardian flats
bracketed by two
Italianate row houses
embody both change
and continuity.

Learning More

Here is a short list of key books and journals on San Francisco Victorians. A few are in print and can be ordered from bookstores; others are rare books available only in research libraries. The best single place to learn about San Francisco Victorians is the San Francisco History and Archives Room of the San Francisco Public Library at Larkin and Grove Streets in the Civic Center. Phone (415) 557-4567 for hours.

In the Victorian Style
Delehanty, Randolph, with photographs by Richard Sexton. San Francisco: Chronicle Books, 1991; paperback edition, 1997. This is the most complete illustrated overview of San Francisco's Victorian houses and includes interiors from parlors to bathrooms.

920 O'Farrell Street: A Jewish Girlhood in Old San Francisco
Levy, Harriet Lane. Berkeley, CA: Heyday Books, 1996. Originally published in 1947, this offers the best room-by-room description of what it was like to live in a San Francisco Victorian row house. Republished with an introduction by Charlene Akers.

Victorian Classics of San Francisco
Brammer, Alex. Sausalito, CA: Windgate Press, 1987. This is a large-format facsimile of the important series on the "Artistic Homes of California" that appeared in the *San Francisco News Letter* in 1887–88.

Picturesque California Homes, No. 1
Newsom, Samuel, and J. Cather Newsom. Los Angeles: Hennessey and Ingalls, 1978. Originally published in San Francisco in 1884–85, this influential pattern book was republished with an introduction by David Gebhard.

Samuel and Joseph Cather Newsom: Victorian Architectural Imagery in California, 1878–1908
Gebhard, David, Harriette Von Breton, and Robert W. Winter. Santa Barbara: University of California, Santa Barbara, Art Museum, 1979. An important monograph on the most exuberant architects active in Victorian California.

"The Real Estate Associates: A Land and Housing Developer of the 1870s"
Bloomfield, Anne. *Journal of the Society of Architectural Historians,* vol. 37, March 1978, pp. 13–33. The best analysis of the business side of row-house development in nineteenth-century San Francisco.

San Francisco: The Ultimate Guide

Delehanty, Randolph. San Francisco: Chronicle Books, 1989; revised edition, 1995. Historical and architectural walking tours including several Victorian neighborhoods.

The Cottage Book

Sexton, Richard. San Francisco: Chronicle Books, 1989. A photographic celebration of San Francisco's Victorian cottages inside and out.

California Architect and Building News

Index by John William Snyder, 1973. This was the single most important architectural journal published in California from 1879 to 1900. Available in the San Francisco History and Archives Room of the San Francisco Public Library.

San Francisco Real Estate Circular

Published by Thomas Magee and his sons from 1866 to 1921, this was the bible of San Francisco real estate brokers in the Victorian era. Available in the San Francisco History and Archives Room of the San Francisco Public Library.

Visitor's Guide

SELECT NORTHERN CALIFORNIA HISTORIC HOUSES

Only two Victorians are open for tours in all of San Francisco: the Octagon House of 1861, and the Haas-Lilienthal House of 1886. The earthquake and fire of 1906 destroyed downtown Victorian San Francisco and its oldest neighborhoods. To see the full spectrum of California Victorians it is necessary to probe beyond San Francisco. For a complete list see Bay Area Historic House Museums, a booklet available by mail from 22701 Main Street, Hayward, CA 94541, or phone (510) 581-0223. Phone individual houses for days, times, and admission fees.

OCTAGON

Octagon House
National Society of the
Colonial Dames of America
2645 Gough Street, at Union
San Francisco, CA 94123
(415) 441-7512

Built in 1861 to standard plans from Orson Squire Fowler's pattern book of 1848, this house is now furnished with colonial and Federal antiques.

GOTHIC REVIVAL

Lachryma Montis
General Vallejo Home
California State Historic Park
20 E. Spain Street
Sonoma, CA 95476
(707) 938-9559

A prefabricated Gothic Revival cottage built in 1850–51, with its original furnishings.

Lathrop House
627 Hamilton Street
Redwood City, CA 94063
(650) 365-5564

A simple Gothic Revival house built in 1863, with period furnishings.

ITALIANATE VILLA

John Muir National Historic Site
National Park Service
4202 Alhambra Avenue
Martinez, CA 94553-3883
(510) 228-8860

An Italianate villa in a garden built in 1883 and furnished by the National Park Service to recreate the period when the famous naturalist lived here.

Pardee Home
672 Eleventh Street
Oakland, CA 94607
(510) 444-2187

An Italianate villa on a half-block site designed in 1868 by Hoagland and Newsom. Contains Pardee family furnishings from around 1900.

ITALIANATE MANSION

Camron-Stanford House
1418 Lakeside Drive
Oakland, CA 94612
(510) 836-1876

Built in 1875 on Lake Merritt in downtown Oakland, this mansion is filled with period furnishings.

GREAT ITALIANATE INTERIOR

Crocker Art Gallery
216 O Street
Sacramento, CA 95814
(916) 264-5423

A superbly restored Italianate private art gallery designed by Seth Babson and built in 1883–84.

EASTLAKE

Cohen-Bray House
1440 Twenty-Ninth Avenue
Oakland, CA 94601
(510) 532-0704

An Eastlake style house built in 1884 with original furnishings.

McConaghy House
18701 Hesperian Boulevard
Hayward, CA 94541
(510) 276-3010

An 1886 Eastlake farmhouse with period furnishings, tank house, and carriage house.

EASTLAKE– QUEEN ANNE

Haas-Lilienthal House
San Francisco Architectural Heritage
2007 Franklin Street
San Francisco, CA 94109
(415) 441-3004

A transitional Eastlake and Queen Anne house designed by Peter R. Schmidt in 1886 containing family furnishings.

FRENCH SECOND EMPIRE

Old Governor's Mansion
1526 H Street
Sacramento, CA 95814
(916) 323-3047

Designed by Nathaniel Goodell in 1877–78 and eclectically furnished.

QUEEN ANNE

Falkirk Cultural Center/ The Robert Dollar Estate
1408 Mission Avenue
San Rafael, CA 94915-1560
(415) 485-3328

Designed by Clinton Day in 1888, the house has period furnishings and a greenhouse. Set in a wooded, eleven-acre estate.

George W. Patterson House
34600 Ardenwood Boulevard
Ardenwood Regional Park
Fremont, CA 94555
(510) 791-4196

Built in 1889, this large house sits in a eucalyptus grove. Ardenwood Regional Park is a 205-acre historic farm with gardens and farm animals.

COLONIAL REVIVAL

Meyers House and Garden Museum

2021 Alameda Avenue
Alameda, CA 94501
(510) 521-1247

Built by and for architect Henry H. Meyers in 1897, this house contains some of its original furnishings.

CLASSICAL REVIVAL

Dunsmuir House and Gardens

2960 Peralta Oaks Court
Oakland, CA 94605
(510) 615-5555

Designed by Eugene Freeman in 1899, this large house contains period furnishings. The forty-acre estate has gardens and a carriage house and milk barn.

BEAUX-ARTS ESTATE

Villa Montalvo Cultural Center

15400 Montalvo Road
P.O. Box 158
Saratoga, CA 95071
(408) 961-5851

A Mediterranean villa designed by William Curlett and built in 1912 for Senator James D. Phelan. It sits in 175 acres nestled against the Santa Cruz Mountains. Only the grounds are open to the public, not the house itself. Phone for musical programs conducted on the grounds.

GEORGIAN REVIVAL ESTATE

Filoli Center

National Trust for Historic Preservation
Cañada Road
Woodside, CA 94062
(650) 364-8300

A baronial estate nestled in the San Francisco watershed and designed by Willis Polk in 1916 for utility baron William Bowers Bourn.

➤ *Haas-Lilienthal House*

HAAS-LILIENTHAL
HOUSE

NEIGHBORHOOD HOUSE TOURS

San Francisco is a city of proud, well-defined neighborhoods with active neighborhood associations. Many of them stage annual house tours. Contact the San Francisco Convention and Visitors Bureau to find out about them:

Visitor Information Center
Hallidie Plaza, 900 Market Street, at Powell Street cable car turn table.
(414) 391-2000

City Walks
Another way to see Victorians, and much else, is through the San Francisco Public Library's City Guides, who conduct walks throughout the city. Phone (415) 557-4266 for information.

PRESERVATION ORGANIZATIONS

San Francisco has two city-wide preservation organizations that conduct tours of vintage houses.

San Francisco Architectural Heritage
The Haas-Lilienthal House
2007 Franklin Street
San Francisco, CA 94109
(415) 441-3004

Heritage conducts walking tours of Pacific Heights on Sundays. There are also tours of the Eastlake–Queen Anne Haas-Lilienthal house, built in 1886.

The Victorian Alliance
4272 Twenty-Fifth Street
San Francisco, CA 94117
(415) 824-2666

About the Photographer

MIKE BLUMENSAADT earned his B.F.A. in photography at the Rochester Institute of Technology and has worked as a photographer in Atlanta and San Francisco. For twenty-two years he has done architectural and travel photography. He has also taught photography and produced many hand made books. His work is in the collections of the High Museum of Art and the Pushkin Museum. He lives in San Francisco and can be contacted at www.matrixphotographics.com.

About the Author

RANDOLPH DELEHANTY, PH.D., is a convention speaker on old and new San Francisco and is the author of eleven books. He holds degrees in history from Georgetown University, the University of Chicago, and Harvard University. Among his books are *In the Victorian Style* and *New Orleans: Elegance and Decadence*, both with photographer Richard Sexton. He has also written *San Francisco: The Ultimate Guide* and *Randolph Delehanty's Ultimate Guide to New Orleans*. He was the founding director of the University of New Orleans' Ogden Museum of Southern Art and is the author of *Art in the American South*. He lives in San Francisco and can be contacted at randolph_delehanty@post.harvard.edu.

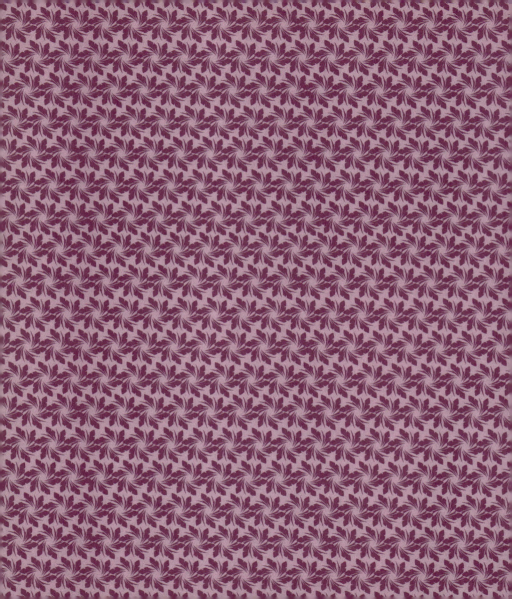